Speaking the

Truth in Love

in a Post-Truth World

SUSAN J. HECK

**Speaking the Truth in Love
in a Post-Truth World**

By Susan J. Heck

© 2020
Focus Publishing, Bemidji, Minnesota
www.focuspublishing.com

Cover design by Amelia Schussman

ISBN 978-1-936141-57-9

Printed in the United States of America

I charge *you* therefore before God and the Lord Jesus Christ,
who will judge the living and the dead at His appearing and His kingdom:
Preach the word!
Be ready in season *and* out of season.

Convince, rebuke, exhort, with all longsuffering and teaching.

For the time will come when they will not endure sound doctrine,
but according to their own desires, because they have itching ears,
they will heap up for themselves teachers;
and they will turn their ears away from the truth, and be turned aside to fables.

2 Timothy 4:1-4

Speaking the Truth in Love in a Post-Truth World

As a pastor's wife of 45 years and a biblical counselor, there is a phrase I have often used with those I counsel. In fact, I have used this phrase probably more than any other phrase. The phrase is this: "Speak the truth in love." It might be the answer I give to a wife who doesn't know how to confront her husband or her child; to a church member who doesn't know how to confront a sinning fellow church member; to an employee who doesn't know how to speak to her boss about an issue at work; to a family member who doesn't know how to speak truth to another family member, extended or close; to an individual who is unjustly accused or confronted; or to a customer who is dealing with a business that is demonstrating a lack of integrity. These are just a few of the scenarios in which speaking truth in love is greatly needed.

There are a number of issues which make speaking the truth in love difficult. I will attempt to clarify and address some of those issues with helpful counsel. But we must admit that, because we live in a post-truth world where truth is no longer regularly spoken, speaking the truth in love is challenging, and certainly not popular, even for a child of God. We are often thought of as archaic, judgmental, profiling, and not relevant to society. Too often, we find ourselves speaking lies instead of truth, appealing to people's emotions rather than their intellect, and being friends of the world rather than friends of Christ.

In this booklet, we will endeavor to answer the following questions:

- What is speaking the truth in love?
- Why must we speak the truth in love?
- Why don't we speak the truth in love?
- Where do we speak the truth in love?
- When do we speak the truth in love?
- How do we speak the truth in love?
- What is the result of speaking the truth in love?

What is Speaking the Truth in Love?

Before we can understand all the particulars of speaking the truth in love, we must first know what it is. When I give counsel to someone, and in that counsel exhort them to speak the truth in love, what exactly am I calling them to do? The phrase "speak the truth in love" comes from Ephesians 4:15. To understand that verse's context, let's consider the passage in its entirety. Ephesians 4:11-16:

> And He Himself gave some to be apostles, some prophets, some evangelists, and some pastors and teachers, for the equipping of the saints for the work of ministry, for the edifying of the body of Christ, till we all come to the unity of the faith and of the knowledge of the Son of God, to a perfect man, to the measure of the stature of the fullness of Christ; that we should no longer be children, tossed to and fro and carried about with every wind of doctrine, by the trickery of men, in the cunning craftiness of deceitful plotting, but, speaking the truth in love, may grow up in all things into Him who is the head — Christ — from whom the whole body, joined and knit together by what every joint supplies, according to the effective working by which every part does its share, causes growth of the body for the edifying of itself in love.

We can see from this passage that Paul is instructing the church at Ephesus regarding spiritual gifts and he lists a number of those gifts. He also states the reasons why we are to use those gifts: to equip the saints to do the work of the ministry, and to edify (or build up) the body of Christ. "Speaking the truth in love," then, includes the idea of using our gifts for equipping and edifying the body of Christ. We must keep in mind that the use of our gifts is not about us but about others and doing what is best for them. So we are to speak truth. We are to speak what is correct doctrine, that which comes from God's Word.

Further, we speak this truth in a spirit of love—agape love—the kind of love that considers the actual needs of those to whom we are speaking. It is certainly possible that, even in speaking the truth in a loving manner, we may risk losing that relationship. But we should be more concerned for their spiritual good than we are for ourselves. We ought to love others enough to warn them of the danger they're in, even if there is a price for us to pay in the process. When we speak the truth to others, giving them loving counsel, we are not to do so from what we think is our own wisdom or our own clever words, but from our Lord's wisdom and His convicting words, a truth which Paul reiterates in 1 Corinthians 2:4-5: **"And my speech and my preaching were not with persuasive words of human wisdom, but in demonstration of the Spirit and of power, that your faith should not be in the wisdom of men but in the power of God."**

Speaking the truth has a 2-fold purpose for God's children. A Christian should always be known as one who speaks the truth at all times. This, of course, comes with a warning of caution. If your friend asks you if her dress makes her look fat, your answer must be truthful, but tempered with love: "Well, I think your blue dress is much more flattering." She will either get what you are saying, or press you further. Then obviously, you must speak the truth.

Our passage teaches the other times we are called to speak truth, and that is when we observe a brother or sister in Christ, who is not effectively **"… working by which every part does is share, causes growth of the body for the edifying of itself in love."** It may be a careless habit of taking the Lord's name in vain; it may be a critical spirit that is obvious as they interact with others; it may be a hint of pride as they perform their God-given gifts; it may be an unforgiving spirit. After giving it much prayer and searching the Scriptures, you believe it is time to "speak the truth in love" to this member of the body of Christ.

Paul goes on in Ephesians 4 to say that we are to speak in this truthful manner with our neighbor, which is not necessarily referring to those who live close to us, though it would include them. The word neighbor could mean anyone, but in this context, it seems to be referring to believers, because Paul goes on to say that we are members one of another, a clear reference to the body of Christ. It ought to be our practice to speak the truth to everyone, whether that person is a fellow believer, a neighbor, or even an enemy. As believers however, we speak the truth to one another because we are members of one another. Paul clearly sets this forth in Ephesians 2 and 3 as he speaks of God's children in terms of being members of a household, a temple, and a body. We belong to each other; therefore, we do not lie to each other. When we lie to one another, whether it is by intentionally verbalizing something that is untrue or by intentionally omitting the truth, it hurts the whole body.

What is speaking the truth in love, then? It is speaking that which is correct doctrinally and that which proceeds from a biblically-committed life to a person who is in need of correction. It is done in love for the benefit of one who needs some adjustment to their attitudes or their actions. A desire to help, prompted by genuine love, is what motivates us to be faithful in this task.

Why Must We Speak the Truth in Love?

Now that we know what speaking the truth in love is, you might be wondering why we must do this. Why should we meddle in another person's life? Perhaps you're thinking, "I have enough problems in my own life and I certainly don't need to be creating more of them."

We've already learned in the previous section that we do this because we love others and we want what is God's best for them. This is not about us; it is about the spiritual welfare of others in the body of Christ. We also do this because it is a command, not only in Ephesians 4, as we've already seen, but also in a number of other passages as well. Matthew 18:15-17 is a command directly from our Lord.

> Moreover if your brother sins against you, go and tell him his fault between you and him alone. If he hears you, you have gained your brother. But if he will not hear, take with you one or two more, that "by the mouth of two or three witnesses every word may be established." And if he refuses to hear them, tell it to the church. But if he refuses even to hear the church, let him be to you like a heathen and a tax collector.

From this passage, we would say that we have a responsibility to speak the truth in love not only because it is a command, but also for the purity of the church. God desires that His bride be holy. When we don't confront a sinning brother, we weaken the resolve of the whole church. A little leaven leavens the whole lump (1 Corinthians 5:6-7).

Another reason for speaking truth in love is found in James 5:19-20: **"Brethren, if anyone among you wanders from the truth, and someone turns him back, let him know that he who turns a sinner from the error of his way will save a soul from death and cover a multitude of sins."**

Saving a soul from death, helping him to turn from the error of his way, is a worthy reason for speaking the truth in love. And James says that we cover a multitude of sins, which means that the sinning stops instead of continuing and being exposed before others.

We must speak the truth in love because it is a command. We must speak the truth in love because if we don't it will affect the purity of the church. And we must speak the truth in love because it has the powerful potential to stop the sinner from continuing their sinful ways and keeping those sins from becoming further exposed. These are marvelous reasons for speaking the truth in love.

Why Don't We Speak the Truth in Love?

One of my concerns for many years has been the lack of biblical confrontation among Christians. Many Christians simply will not do the right thing when it comes to lovingly speaking the truth to those who are in sin. Instead, those who know of an offense will often gossip about the person or tell the pastor or his wife in hopes that they will take care of it. Many times, they avoid the person altogether or become bitter or resentful, even hating them in their heart. These are all wrong and sinful ways of handling offenses. We must do the right thing, as we've already seen.

Why is it that we don't speak the truth in love? Why do we allow offenses to go on for so long? Perhaps the main reason we don't speak the truth in love is fear of man. We are afraid of losing friendships or straining relationships. Unfortunately, this just compounds our own sin. In Galatians 1:10, Paul warns us that if we are man-pleasers, we are not servants of Christ. He writes: **"For do I now persuade men, or God? Or do I seek to please men? For if I still pleased men, I would not be a bondservant of Christ."** Jesus warns even more boldly in Luke 12:4-5:

> And I say to you, my friends, do not be afraid of those who kill the body, and after that have no more that they can do. But I will show you whom you should fear: Fear Him who, after He has killed, has power to cast into hell; yes, I say to you, fear Him!

I remember doing a word study on fear years ago and discovering that we are not to fear anyone but God (with the exception of one command to fear our parents). Fear of man is a sin, and one we must put off so that we are free to help those who need a word of admonishment.

Another reason we don't speak to others when it is needed is because of fear of rejection. It's possible that we'll be labeled as judgmental or self-righteous. If that does happen, we can take great comfort in the words of Peter regarding our Lord Jesus, in 1 Peter 2:21-24:

> For to this you were called, because Christ also suffered for us, leaving us an example, that you should follow His steps: Who committed no sin, nor was deceit found in His mouth; who, when He was reviled, did not revile in return; when He suffered, He did not threaten, but committed Himself to Him who judges righteously.

We can take great comfort in the reality that our Lord was rejected too. We can commit ourselves to the One who judges righteously. We can cast all our cares on Him because we know He cares for us.

Another reason we don't speak the truth in love is because we fear not knowing what to say. While this concern is legitimate, it's one that can be easily remedied by being prepared. Paul is clear in Romans 15:14 that all believers are able to help each other in this area: **"Now I myself am confident concerning you, my brethren, that you also are full of goodness, filled with all knowledge, able also to admonish one another."** We must do the disciplined work of studying the Scriptures so that we know how to approach each person's situation. Paul speaks of this need to be prepared in 2 Timothy 2:15: **"Be diligent to present yourself approved to God, a worker who does not need to be ashamed, rightly dividing the word of truth."** This means I must know what God says about the issues before I admonish another. What does God say about sexual sin; harsh husbands; not paying your taxes; businesses who lie about their products; wives who are not submissive to their husbands; anger issues; unforgiveness; drunkenness; homosexuality; and employees who are lazy? These are just a few of the issues that might need to be addressed in the life of another believer. Would you know how to lovingly admonish someone caught up in one of these sins? Do you know what God says about each of these issues? Because the Word of God is sufficient for life and godliness, there is no reason for us not to be prepared. We are competent to counsel, but we must know what the Word of God says so that we know how to appropriately address each situation. We must not refrain from speaking the truth in love because we fear man, we fear rejection, or we fear not knowing what to say.

Where Do We Speak the Truth in Love?

Another common question we need to consider is, "Where do I do this?" Is this something I am commanded to do just in my home or with those in my church? Do I really take care of all offenses in this way? The answer to that last question is yes, we do this as much as possible. Paul put it well in Acts 24:16: **"This being so, I myself always strive to have a conscience without offense toward God and men."** And in Romans 12:18, he admonishes us: **"If it is possible, as much as depends on you, live peaceably with all men."** With that in mind, the answer to where we are to speak the truth in love will be answered in four categories. We do this in our hearts, in our homes, in our houses of worship, and in our hostile world.

1. <u>We must speak the truth in love to our own hearts.</u> Proverbs 27:19 wisely says: **"As in water face reflects a face, so a man's heart reveals the man."** How can we help someone else if we aren't being honest with ourselves first? We need to make sure that we are clearly seeing the issues as sinful offenses, and we are not clouded by bitterness or resentment. Have we taken a good look in the mirror and done some thorough self-examination? How can we help our brother get the speck out of his eye if we haven't first cleared the beam out of our own eye? Jesus is clear in Matthew 7:1-5:

> Judge not, that you be not judged. For with what judgment you judge, you will be judged; and with the measure you use, it will be measured back to you. And why do you look at the speck in your brother's eye, but do not consider the plank in your own eye? Or how can you say to your brother, "Let me remove the speck from your eye"; and look, a plank is in your own eye? Hypocrite! First remove the plank from your own eye, and then you will see clearly to remove the speck from your brother's eye.

Jesus is also clear in Matthew 12:34-36 that our hearts speaks what is truly in them:

> Brood of vipers! How can you, being evil, speak good things? For out of the abundance of the heart the mouth speaks. A good man out of the good treasure of his heart brings forth good things, and an evil man out of the evil treasure brings forth evil things.

To properly examine our own hearts, we must speak the truth to our own hearts, and that requires, again, that we know what the truth of God's Word says about the matter at hand. Once we have done the self-examination about our own personal sin and are confident that we have pure motives, we are ready to prayerfully and humbly approach our brother or sister in the Lord.

2. <u>We must speak the truth in love in our homes.</u> This certainly does not mean that I have to speak my mind on every subject that comes up in a given day; a wise person will taste their words before they speak them. But it does mean that if a child or a spouse or anyone else living in the home has an ongoing pattern of wrong attitudes or actions, then we are to speak the truth to them in love. And, yes, this includes a wife to her husband. Often, I hear from well-meaning Christians the erroneous notion that wives are never to confront their spouses. I'm not sure where that idea came from, but certainly not from the Word of God. In Matthew 18:15, Jesus is clear that if a brother offends you, you are to go to them about it, and He does not include an exception clause. He doesn't say you go unless it's your husband, and then you don't go. Likewise, this command also applies to children. We are told in numerous passages that children are to obey their parents in the Lord. If a child does not obey his or her parent's word, then not only does that parent need to speak to the child, but they also need to discipline the child (see Ephesians 6:1; Colossians 3:20; Proverbs 19:18). I am convinced that Christian homes are in bad shape today for many reasons, but one of those reasons is a refusal to take care of offenses. We would rather hate our spouse or our child in our heart than to do the right thing. We would rather avoid them or lash out in anger than to do the right thing. But Leviticus 19:17 speaks directly to this issue: **"You shall not hate your brother in your heart. You shall surely rebuke your neighbor, and not bear sin because of him."**

3. <u>We must speak the truth in love in our houses of worship.</u> This would include anyone who belongs to the body of believers. It doesn't have to be to someone who attends your local church gathering, but any believer in Christ who is sinning. We have cited Matthew 18 already, so suffice it to say that when there is an offense, we have a responsibility to go to that person. If they repent after we've spoken to them concerning their sin, great; if not, then we go again. In fact, the Greek text indicates that we might have to go repeatedly. If there is still no repentance after multiple conversations, we then get two or three others involved, in hopes that this will bring the sinning brother or sister to their knees. If there is still no repentance, then both the sin and the sinner are told to the church. The church then prayerfully and lovingly counsels them in hopes of leading them to repentance. If the sinning brother or sister continues to refuse to repent, then they are to be put out of the church.

It's also important that we not put the "going" part off; we must do it in a timely manner, being certain, of course, that we have first examined our own hearts. Jesus is clear in Matthew 5:23-24:

> Therefore if you bring your gift to the altar, and there remember that your brother has something against you, leave your gift there before the altar, and go your way. First be reconciled to your brother, and then come and offer your gift.

We are to take care of offenses as soon as possible. It is heartbreaking to see those who put off the going part and instead put on the gossip part or the get-angry and get-bitter part. This is not right and it is not pleasing to the Lord.

4. <u>We must speak the truth in love in our hostile world.</u> (Notice that when you put these four places together, it encompasses all people.) Now, just to be very clear, please know that practicing this will no doubt incur persecution and hatred. Jesus has given us full warning of this in John 15:18-25:

> If the world hates you, you know that it hated Me before it hated you. If you were of the world, the world would love its own. Yet because you are not of the world, but I chose you out of the world, therefore the world hates you.

> Remember the word that I said to you, "A servant is not greater than his master." If they persecuted Me, they will also persecute you. If they kept My word, they will keep yours also. But all these things they will do to you for My name's sake, because they do not know Him who sent Me. If I had not come and spoken to them, they would have no sin, but now they have no excuse for their sin. He who hates Me hates My Father also. If I had not done among them the works which no one else did, they would have no sin; but now they have seen and also hated both Me and My Father. But this happened that the word might be fulfilled which is written in their law, "They hated Me without a cause."

Jesus faithfully spoke to unbelievers about their sin and He makes clear that they hated Him because of it. My friend, when you lovingly confront an unbeliever about their sin, they will, more than likely, hate you and persecute you for it. In fact, John the Baptist was beheaded for speaking the truth to Herod. Read the following with careful thought. Matthew 14:1-12:

> At that time Herod the tetrarch heard the report about Jesus and said to his servants, "This is John the Baptist; he is risen from the dead, and therefore these powers are at work in him." For Herod had laid hold of John and bound him, and put him in prison for the sake of Herodias, his brother Philip's wife. Because John had said to him, "It is not lawful for you to have her." And although he wanted to put him to death, he feared the multitude, because they counted him as a prophet. But when Herod's birthday was celebrated, the daughter of Herodias danced before them and pleased Herod. Therefore he promised with an oath to give her whatever she might ask. So she, having been prompted by her mother, said, "Give me John the Baptist's head here on a platter." And the king was sorry; nevertheless, because of the oaths and because of those who sat with him, he commanded it to be given to her. So he sent and had John beheaded in prison. And his head was brought on a platter and given to the girl, and she brought it to her mother. Then his disciples came and took away the body and buried it, and went and told Jesus.

When John told Herod that it wasn't lawful for him to have Phillip's wife, John was speaking the truth in love—and it cost him his head, it cost him his life. You're not likely to face anything that drastic, but it will probably still cost you. But, as Peter says in 1 Peter 3:17: **"…it is better, if it is the will of God, to suffer for doing good than for doing evil."**

Where do we speak the truth in love? We speak the truth in our hearts, in our homes, in our houses of worship, and in our hostile world.

When Do We Speak the Truth in Love?

As we consider the timing of when we should speak the truth in love, it must first be said that we are to do it quickly, as we've noted already. It isn't for us to wait until we find a convenient time; if we do that, it's likely that we'll never get around to speaking to another about their sin. Paul admonishes his son in the faith, Timothy, in 2 Timothy 4:2, to **"Preach the word! Be ready in season and out of season. Convince, rebuke, exhort, with all longsuffering and teaching."** Inherent in preaching the Word is the responsibility of speaking divine truth. This truth, that is, the very Word of God, is to be heralded. This truth, that is God-breathed and is all-authoritative and all-sufficient, is to be proclaimed. It is this Word that gives us sound doctrine, rebukes our sin, corrects our wrong thinking, instructs us in righteousness, and grows us by making us complete, fully equipped for every good work. These words—the Word of God—are the words we are to use when confronting another in love. The Bible is living and powerful and sharper than a two-edged sword (Hebrews 4:12); no other book or person has such depth and wisdom.

Paul also tells us the "when" of heralding this truth. He says we are to be ready in season and out of season. That is, we should be ready in a moment's notice. It might be a convenient time, or it might be an inconvenient time. Regardless, we are to be ready. And having told us to be ready, Paul then goes on to outline for us a helpful progression of what is involved when we speak the truth in love. He begins by saying that we first convince, or reprove, others of their sin. Instead of diminishing sin and justifying it, a believer must love others enough to point out the truth of their sin. Again, we preach the Word! It is the inspired Word of God that holds up a mirror to expose our sin and our error.

Once we have pointed out the error biblically, then Paul says we rebuke. This is a command to admonish those who will not let go of their sin. Some may bristle at the word rebuke, but we should not, as it is in the very Word of God. It is the right and loving thing to do. Jesus loves us and He rebukes us out of love.

Once we have reproved them and shown them from the Word of God that what they are doing is sinful or that they are in some sort of error, then we must forbid them to continue in that sin or error. They have to let go of it or it will master them. We aren't to minimize their sin, but to tell them the danger of their sin. I remember several years ago a young woman came to me for counseling. She told me she had been to several "Christian counselors" before coming to me, and yet, I was the first to tell her that she was in sin. What a blight on the Christian counselors of our day, but more so a slight on God and His Word, which has power to change lives. When we rightly call something sin, there is always hope because God has provided a remedy for sin in His Word. But when we psychologize it or minimize it or call it something else, there's no hope because there's no remedy.

After we have reproved and rebuked, then Paul says we exhort. To exhort is to bring comfort. We should never leave someone discouraged after a reproof and a rebuke; instead, we ought always to give hope through the Word. Our sins are often binding, but the Word of God has the answers that will free us from those sins. Passage after passage offers us help not only in knowing what sins we are to put off, but also in what virtues we are to put on instead. As we reprove and rebuke and exhort from these powerful and life-changing words of God, Paul says we are to do all these things with longsuffering and teaching, or doctrine, as your translation might read. Earlier in that same epistle, in 2 Timothy 2:24-26, Paul admonished Timothy regarding this important truth:

> And a servant of the Lord must not quarrel but be gentle to all, able to teach, patient, in humility correcting those who are in opposition, if God perhaps will grant them repentance, so that they may know the truth, and that they may come to their senses and escape the snare of the devil, having been taken captive by him to do his will.

We see in this passage that Paul couples the concepts of teaching and patience just as he does in chapter four of the same epistle. He writes a similar idea in 1 Thessalonians 5:14: **"Now we exhort you, brethren, warn those who are unruly, comfort the fainthearted, uphold the weak, be patient with all."** The idea here is that as we warn the unruly, comfort those who are fainthearted, and support the weak, we are to treat everyone with patience, even as we refuse to compromise doctrine. In all of our efforts to correct sin or error, there is no need to be brash or rude. We do these things, Paul says in 2 Timothy 4:2, with longsuffering, with forbearance.

A number of years ago, a woman approached me at a conference during a break between sessions. I could tell that she was angry; she was visibly shaking, and she wanted to speak to me outside. I hesitated, because my practice is to not speak with conference attendees without a witness present, but I saw that everyone was busy chatting or at the book table, so I agreed. To my surprise, she had this very verse, 2 Timothy 4:2, in her hand and pointed her finger at it and then at me and said, "I am going to rebuke you!" I won't go into all the details, but she was clearly out of control, even grabbing me by the arms and physically shaking me. It was one of those I-can't-believe-this-is-happening moments. I was able to diffuse the situation, thanks be to God, and get back inside. But, thinking back on the situation now, I wish I had recalled the part of this verse that she forgot, to convince and rebuke and exhort "with all longsuffering and teaching." She practiced neither.

The wonderful thing about following the principles laid out in this verse is that it is the Holy Spirit who acts as the Great Convincer and Convicter of sin. Our responsibility is simply to deliver the truth; He is the one who does the work of convincing and convicting. This does not mean that we will never need to rebuke people sharply. There are times, especially when dealing with false teachers, that we must reject them, avoid them, and even rebuke them sharply, but this would come after several warnings. Among those in need of a sharp rebuke are those who are involved in sexual sin; Scripture tells us to flee, that it should not even be named among God's people (see 1 Corinthians 6:18 and Ephesians 5:3).

It must be noted that there are those who are endeavoring to put away habitual sins—anger, unwholesome language, and the like—and we must exhibit longsuffering and patience in the changing process. People don't change overnight. Paul puts it beautifully in 2 Corinthians 3:18: **"But we** all, with unveiled face, beholding as in a mirror the glory of the Lord, are being transformed into the same image from glory to glory, just as by the Spirit of the Lord." As we exercise patience in the waiting process, we do so by continually reminding those we're helping what the Scripture says regarding their sin or error. And while Paul doesn't say it in this text, we ought to be praying while we're waiting! Pray for their hearts to be softened by the truth. Pray that their repentance will be thorough.

We not only do this with patience, but also with teaching, which could be translated as pure doctrine. We tell them what God says about their sin or error. We don't minimize it or rationalize it, but we give them the truth in love. It's interesting that Paul starts this verse with a call to preach the Word and ends it with an appeal to sound doctrine. Like two slices of bread, so to speak, we begin with the Word and we end with doctrine. The inner makings of this sandwich, then, are the diligence to do this when it's convenient and when it's not, and the willingness to convince, rebuke and exhort with all longsuffering, and we do it promptly.

How Do We Speak the Truth in Love?

Perhaps you are wondering how you should approach someone about an issue. I strongly encourage you to give this much prayer before, during, and after your conversation with them. Pray beforehand that God will open their heart to hear truth, praying while you're speaking that your words will not fall on deaf ears or a hard heart, and pray afterward that the dear Holy Spirit will do the work of conviction of sin and lead them to repentance.

Coupled with prayer must be patience. Again, Paul writes, in 1 Thessalonians 5:14: "**Now we exhort you, brethren, warn those who are unruly, comfort the fainthearted, uphold the weak, be patient with all.**" He also writes in Galatians 6:1: "**Brethren, if a man is overtaken in any trespass, you who are spiritual restore such a one in a spirit of gentleness, considering yourself lest you also be tempted.**" Our confrontation of others is to be done with meekness and humility. Often, I will say in the counseling room, "I am coming to you today out of love regarding this issue in your life, and I hope that you too will love me enough to come to me when I am in need of correction."

In 2 Timothy 2:24, Paul writes: "**... and a servant of the Lord must not**

quarrel but be gentle to all, able to teach, patient." The words "must not" mean that this is our moral obligation. It is our moral obligation to not quarrel, to not dispute or fight with others. You can read through all the pages of the Gospel accounts—Matthew, Mark, Luke, and John—and you will not find our Lord quarreling. You will see Him speak truth in love and sometimes in righteous anger, but He does not quarrel, and neither should we. We must contend for the faith, but we must not strive and argue. We must speak truth in love.

Now, there are some examples of heated disagreements in the Scriptures. Paul speaks in Galatians 2 of reproving Peter to his face, but he says he did so because it was necessary; Peter had become fearful of eating with the Gentiles and Paul knew it was wrong. In Acts 15, Barnabas and Paul contended over whether to take Mark on a missionary journey. Paul refused to take Mark along because Mark had failed to do the work he should have done, so they departed and went their separate ways. In Philippians 4:2, Paul mentions that Euodia and Syntyche were upset with one another over something and he urged others in the church to get involved in order to help them. I bring up these examples as illustrations of people in the Scriptures who had issues with one another, but who dealt with those issues or had someone else come alongside them to help them. Christians are not exempt from the temptation to quarrel, but we must do what Paul tells the church at Colosse to do in Colossians 3:13: "… **bearing with one another, and forgiving one another, if anyone has a complaint against another; even as Christ forgave you, so you also must do.**" In this verse, complaint is the same word as quarrel. We must forgive and we must endeavor to keep peace with one another.

Instead of quarreling, we must be gentle. To be gentle means to be mild or kind. It's the same Greek word that Paul uses in 1 Thessalonians 2:7 when he describes his care for the church at Thessalonica. He puts it like this: "**But we were gentle among you, just as a nursing mother cherishes her own children.**" Nursing mothers are kind and mild toward their babies; they certainly don't quarrel with them. In fact, it would be foolish for a mother to do so, because her baby wouldn't even know what she was saying. A baby simply can't understand. Gentleness is the virtue we must put on when we're dealing with others. This does not mean that we ignore their sin; it does mean that we are gentle and kind when we address them. We must confront with humility.

Speaking the truth in love doesn't mean it is *always* done with a mild tone or a quiet voice (see 1 Corinthians 4:21). Even Jesus spoke the truth in love with the money changers, and He was angry when He did so. Matthew 21:12-13 records for us:

> Then Jesus went into the temple of God and drove out all those who bought and sold in the temple, and overturned the tables of the money changers and the seats of those who sold doves. And He said to them, "It is written, 'My house shall be called a house of prayer,' but you have made it a 'den of thieves.'"

Paul was also a bit firm with Peter when Peter wouldn't eat with the Gentiles. Peter's behavior was having a sinful effect on others, as we see in Galatians 2:11-13:

> Now when Peter had come to Antioch, I withstood him to his face, because he was to be blamed; for before certain men came from James, he would eat with the Gentiles; but when they came, he withdrew and separated himself, fearing those who were of the circumcision. And the rest of the Jews also played the hypocrite with him, so that even Barnabas was carried away with their hypocrisy."

Most of the time, a gentle voice is the best approach. Proverbs 15:1-2 reminds us: **"A soft answer turns away wrath, but a harsh word stirs up anger. The tongue of the wise uses knowledge rightly, but the mouth of fools pours forth foolishness."** A firmer tone, even a raised voice or a righteously angry voice, might be what is needed, depending on the circumstance. For example, consider a child to whom you have given a command, who refuses to obey. You have disciplined him, but he goes right back to the same act of disobedience. In this situation, a firmer tone of voice will be more effective.

How do we speak the truth in love? We speak with gentleness and with humility, all the while examining ourselves. We also bathe our endeavors in much prayer. Some more practical "how to" examples can be found at the end of this booklet.

What is the Result of Speaking the Truth in Love?

When we stop to consider the potential results of speaking the truth in love, we ought to be motivated to do it more often. Paul gives us several results that come from speaking the truth in love. He puts it like this, in 2 Timothy 2:25-26: **"In humility correcting those who are in opposition, if God perhaps will grant them repentance, so that they may know the truth, and that they may come to their senses and escape the snare of the devil, having been taken captive by him to do his will."** Humility is the idea of meekness, which means to have strength under control. Moses was said to be the meekest man in all the earth. In Numbers 12:3 we read: **"Now the man Moses was very humble, more than all men who were on the face of the earth."** It would do us well to review Moses' life and learn from him how to deal with people. He not only faced the Sons of Korah in their rebellion, but he also dealt with Pharaoh and his opposition numerous times. He maintained a spirit of meekness through 40 years of wandering through the wilderness with the rebellious Israelites. We can learn much from his example.

Now, is there good fruit that can come from being humble when exhorting others? What is that fruit? The first fruit mentioned in 2 Timothy 2:25-26 is repentance. Repentance is essentially a reversal of the issues for which the individual is being confronted. It is that person turning away from their sin and turning toward obedience. It could also result in repentance unto salvation, especially when we consider that the one we're approaching might still be lost in sin. In fact, Paul goes on to say that they might know the truth. This would refer to that which is true to what God says. For example, if the one we're addressing is in error about the gospel, thinking that the gospel is health, wealth and prosperity, it's possible that our speaking the truth in love will result in their understanding the truth of the Lordship of Christ and the need to deny themselves. If they are in error about baptism, as Apollos was in Acts 18, it's quite possible they will be brought into the truth about baptism. If they are in error about women preaching to men, they may be brought into truth about that. If they are in error about women being submissive to their husbands, they may be brought into truth about that. These are just a few examples of how speaking the truth in love may result in repentance, helping someone to learn that truth.

Our desire in all of this is for people to know the truth so that God may be glorified. His name and the reputation of His church are at stake. I was made aware of this again just recently, as I had several people challenge me on some issues. One couple responded back to me, not necessarily in agreement with my answers, but thanking me for responding and for doing it graciously. Argumentative people shut doors for helpful communication, but if we speak the truth in love, we will find that it often opens the door for helpful dialogue, and some will come to repentance and the knowledge of the truth because of it.

Paul mentions another result of speaking the truth in love: that the person we are speaking to may come to their senses. This means that they will change their thinking as one awakened out of a deep sleep. Perhaps this was what Paul had in mind when he wrote to the church at Ephesus in Ephesians 5:14: **"Therefore He says: 'Awake, you who sleep, arise from the dead, and Christ will give you light.'"**

Another result that comes from correcting others with humility is that they may escape the snare of the devil. The snare of the devil is a reference to his tricks. We must not forget that he is like a roaring lion seeking whom he may devour (1 Peter 5:8). He's like a lion that wants to hunt, steal, and kill his prey. He's behind all lies and all that is false, so he certainly does not want those who are duped into his tactics to be awakened out of their slumber. In fact, Paul ends this verse saying that they have been taken captive by the devil to do his will. They were in such a stupor that they did not realize they were being held captive by the evil one. We must, as servants of Christ and good soldiers of His, do battle with the evil one, for there are many whose minds are being held captive by him.

When we put all these things together, we see that some truly wonderful things can come about from our efforts at speaking the truth in love: repentance, knowledge of the truth, coming to one's senses, and escaping the snare of the evil one. My friend, these are excellent results! As we endeavor to speak the truth to those who are in need of it, our prayer and hope should always be that repentance and restoration of relationships will take place.

Having said that, we must also be realistic and know that doing the right thing, speaking the truth in love, does not always produce the results we desire. But this is a good indicator that we are doing the right thing. Paul makes this clear in 2 Timothy 3:12 when he writes: **"Yes, and all who**

desire to live godly in Christ Jesus will suffer persecution." This statement is not a possibility but an absolute. If you haven't been persecuted for your faith yet, no worries, you will; Paul says it's a promise. But it's also possible, if you've been a Christian for long and you've still never suffered persecution that you might need to examine whether you are walking in a holy manner. Such suffering for Christ is not a curse but a gift. Consider what Paul writes to the church at Philippi in Philippians 1:29: **"For to you it has been granted on behalf of Christ, not only to believe in Him, but also to suffer for His sake."** Some people flee from persecution and do everything they can do to avoid it. But godly men and women know that it will come, and they embrace it because they know that their Lord suffered too. If you are rejected and persecuted and hated for doing the right thing, consider it a privilege to bear the name of the One who gave you life eternal. Don't shy away from controversy or speaking up when there is incorrect doctrine being taught or wrong behavior being exhibited. Do not fear the persecution you may receive because of it. Do not be afraid, my friend, for it is a wonderful opportunity to prove your loyalty to your Lord and to draw ever so close to Him.

This booklet is by no means exhaustive, but it is meant to be helpful. "Speaking the truth in love" is certainly a popular phrase which is used often in Christian circles, but I wonder if we are actually doing it effectively for the glory of God? Speaking the truth in love in a post-truth world is at times challenging, but a wise Christian will remember the wisdom of Solomon's words in Proverbs 8:7: **"For my mouth will speak truth; wickedness is an abomination to my lips."**

Some Examples of Right and Wrong Ways to Confront

<u>Wrong:</u> Hands on hips, raised voice, you abruptly say, "I want to talk to you *now*!"
<u>Right:</u> Walking prayerfully, with a gentle voice, you say, "Do you have some time to talk with me?"

<u>Wrong:</u> "You are consistently leaving your dirty clothes on the floor and frankly, I am quite sick of it!"
<u>Right:</u> "Is there something I can do to encourage you to pick up your clothes? It's becoming quite a challenge for me to keep a good attitude about this."

<u>Wrong:</u> "If you don't stop this sinful anger, I am going to the pastor to have you put out of the church!"
<u>Right:</u> "Honey, I've noticed your anger is becoming more frequent. I am really concerned for your soul, because the Word of God is clear that ongoing anger is a sin worthy of eternal punishment. Can we go together to get some help?

<u>Wrong:</u> "If you don't lower my bill and stop deceiving your customers, I'm going to stop my service with you! You guys are nothing but wicked pagans!"
<u>Right:</u> "I am trying to understand why our bill keeps going up every month. It seems I have to call often and get it lowered. The last person I spoke to told me something different than you just did."

Questions for Further Help

1. What if my authority figure (husband, pastor, etc.) doesn't think I should confront (speak the truth in love to) an individual?

   You should ask them for biblical evidence that this is not the right thing to do. Find out their reasons. Then if, after you have talked with them, you are still convinced by the Word of God that this is a situation that needs to be addressed, graciously tell your spouse or pastor that you must obey God over man (Acts 5:29).

2. What if my husband is violent or verbally abusive and I am fearful to say anything to him, even though it needs to be said?

   In this situation, I would do confrontation in a public place and have a friend or pastor nearby. I would also call 911 if there is any physical abuse and make use of any legal protections that are available.

3. What if I am unsure that an individual should be spoken to regarding a certain matter?

   If you are unsure whether a situation merits confrontation, it might be wise for you to first confide in an older, godlier man or woman, a pastor, or an elder. Get their wise counsel before proceeding.

4. What if I have done the right thing, spoken the truth in love, and nothing changes, or the person avoids me and gossips about me?

   I would certainly bathe the situation in prayer, and even consider fasting and prayer. If they are avoiding you and gossiping about you, then you should go again and speak the truth in love. You may also need to involve others at this juncture.

5. What if I have done this in the past (spoken the truth in love) and now I realize that I have done it all wrong?

The righteous thing to do would be to go back to the person and ask for forgiveness for the way in which you handled the situation. Perhaps you could express to that person what you have learned about how to correctly speak the truth in love and then offer to them what you think would have been a more loving and God-honoring approach.

Questions to Consider

1. When you are trying to help someone with a problem in their life, which term describes you more often: "gentle" or "argumentative"?

2. How can one put off being argumentative?

3. What things have been helpful to you in your efforts to correct others in love?

4. How could you use the information you have learned from this booklet to confront an abusive husband; a wayward child; a sinning church member; someone who is a gossip; a strained relationship; or someone you do business with who has lied to you?

5. What can you learn from Jesus' examples of speaking the truth in love, in John 2:13-17; John 4:1-45; and John 8:12-59?

6. What are some other examples in Scripture of correct ways to handle offenses and incorrect ways to handle offenses? Spend some time studying these examples and record the things you have learned and the principles you can use in your own life when speaking the truth in love.